Building Your Nursing Career

A Guide for Students

Second Edition

Building Your Nursing Career
A Guide for Students

Second Edition

JANICE WADDELL, RN, PhD

GAIL J. DONNER, RN, PhD

MARY M. WHEELER, RN, MEd

An Affiliate of Elsevier

An Affiliate of Elsevier

Copyright © 2004, Elsevier Canada, a division of Harcourt Canada Ltd.

All rights reserved. No part of this publication may be reproduced or transmitted in any form or by any means, electronic or mechanical, including photocopy, recording, or any information storage and retrieval system, without permission in writing from the publisher. Reproducing passages from this book without such written permission is an infringement of copyright law.

Requests for permission to make any copies of any part of the work should be mailed to: College Licensing Officer, access ©, 1 Yonge Street, Suite 1900, Toronto, ON, M5E 1E5. Fax: (416) 868-1621. All other inquiries should be directed to the publisher.

Every reasonable effort has been made to acquire permission for copyright material used in this text, and to acknowledge all such indebtedness accurately. Any errors and omissions called to the publisher's attention will be corrected in future printings.

National Library of Canada Cataloguing in Publication Data

Waddell, Janice, date.
    Building your nursing career / Janice Waddell, Gail J. Donner, Mary M. Wheeler. – 2nd ed.

ISBN 0-920513-51-4

    1. Nursing–Vocational guidance. 2. Career development. I. Donner, Gail J. (Gail Judith), date. Wheeler, Mary M. III. Title.

RT82.W32 2004   610.73'06' 9   C2003-904165-4

Acquisitions Editor: Ann Millar
Development Editor: Eliza Marciniak
Publishing Services Manager: Deborah L. Vogel
Senior Project Manager: Jodi M. Willard
Design Manager: Mark Bernard

Elsevier Canada
1 Goldthorne Ave., Toronto, ON, Canada M8Z 5S7
Phone: 1-866-896-3331
Fax: 1-866-359-9534

This book was printed in U.S.A.
2 3 4 5   08 07 06 05 04

REVIEWERS

Faculty Reviewers

Lynda Atack
Centennial College,
Toronto, Ontario

Marilyn Beaton
Memorial University of Newfoundland,
St John's, Newfoundland and Labrador

Gail Tomblin Murphy
Dalhousie University,
Halifax, Nova Scotia

Elizabeth Polakoff
Red River College,
Winnipeg, Manitoba

Darlene Steven
Lakehead University,
Thunder Bay, Ontario

Student Reviewers

Melissa Furfaro
Student,
McMaster University,
Hamilton, Ontario

Heidi Hofstra
Student,
University of Edmonton,
Edmonton, Alberta

Kristina Kolodziej
Student,
McMaster University,
Hamilton, Ontario

ABOUT THE AUTHORS

Janice Waddell, RN, PhD, is an Associate Professor at the School of Nursing, Ryerson University, Toronto, Ontario. She is currently the Associate Director for the Basic and Collaborative Nursing Degree Programs at Ryerson. Janice's clinical expertise is in the areas of adolescent and child mental health and bereavement counselling. Her research foci include career planning and development for nurses, with a particular emphasis on student nurses, and the experience of children who have witnessed family violence. She teaches nursing courses that focus on current professional issues and trends, and she supervises senior nursing students in their final clinical placement experiences. Janice has facilitated numerous student-focused career planning and development workshops within Ontario. She has been an Associate of donnerwheeler since 1994.

Gail J. Donner, RN, PhD, has recently completed her appointment as the Dean of the Faculty of Nursing at University of Toronto (1999-2001). She has been involved in major nursing research projects, has written numerous academic journal articles, and has contributed to various books, including Baumgart: Canadian Nursing Facing the Future (Mosby, 1998). She has consulted on various career development projects, including a resource manual for the preparation of nurse career coaches that was launched at the International Council of Nurses Congress in Copenhagen in June 2001.

Mary M. Wheeler, RN, MEd, is the partner in their career development consultant company (donnerwheeler) and has worked with Gail on numerous projects in addition to this text. She taught at Ryerson in leadership and change, communication, and teaching, and she was Interim Executive Director/Director of Member Programs and Coordinator of Professional Issues at RNAO from 1986 to 1991. She has primarily focused on the consultant position since 1991.

Mary and Gail have been involved in career planning and development work for more than 10 years. Their work includes individual and organizational consulting, workshops, an online program (currently being piloted), and research and publishing in career development. They have developed their own model for career planning and professional development, incorporating five phases for identifying and assessing the current environment and developing a realistic plan for the future. They have developed career planning programs for Toronto's Women's College Hospital and Hospital for Sick Children and received a great deal of interest when they presented their Model at the International Council of Nurses conference in July 2001.

CONTENTS

CHAPTER 1 CAREER PLANNING AND DEVELOPMENT AS A STUDENT ACTIVITY, 1

How to Use Your Student Guide, 2
Career Planing and Development, 3
Why Career Planning and Development Is Important for Nursing Students, 3
The Donner-Wheeler Career Planning and Development Model, 4

2 PLANNING YOUR CAREER, 7

Phase One: Scanning Your Environment, 7
What Is Scanning?, 7
Why Is Scanning Important?, 8
How and When Do You Scan?, 8
ACTIVITY 1: SCANNING YOUR ENVIRONMENT, 10
What Have You Accomplished?, 14
What Is Your Next Step?, 14

Phase Two: Completing Your Self-Assessment and Reality Check, 14
What Is Self-Assessment?, 14
Why Is Assessing Yourself Important?, 14
Beginning the Self-Assessment Process, 15
ACTIVITY 2: COMPLETING YOUR SELF-ASSESSMENT, 20
Your Reality Check, 26
ACTIVITY 3: REALITY CHECK, 27
What Have You Accomplished?, 29
What Is Your Next Step?, 29

Phase Three: Creating Your Career Vision, 29
What Is a Career Vision?, 29
Why Should I Have a Career Vision?, 29
How to Create Your Own Career Vision, 30
ACTIVITY 4: CREATING YOUR CAREER VISION, 32
What Have You Accomplished?, 34
What Is Your Next Step?, 34

Phase Four: Developing Your Strategic Career Plan, 34
What Are Career Plans?, 34
Why Should I Develop a Career Plan?, 34
How Should I Plan?, 34
ACTIVITY 5: DEVELOPING YOUR STRATEGIC CAREER PLAN, 37
Thinking of Graduate Studies?, 38
What Have You Accomplished?, 39
What Is Your Next Step?, 39

Phase Five: Marketing Yourself, 39
Student Nurses as Self-Marketers, 39
Why Marketing Yourself Is Important, 39
How Can I Market Myself?, 39
ACTIVITY 6: MARKETING YOURSELF, 46
What Have You Accomplished?, 48

What Next?, 48

3 CHOOSING YOUR FIRST JOB AS A REGISTERED NURSE, 49

Your Environmental Scan, 49
Your Self-Assessment, 49
Your Career Vision, 50
Your Strategic Career Plan, 50
Marketing, 50

4 DO YOU NEED MORE HELP?, 51

CAREER PLANNING AND DEVELOPMENT RESOURCES, 53

Appendix A   Samples of Student Résumés, 55

Student Entering Third Year of Baccalaureate Program Seeking Clinical Placement in a Maternal Child Setting, 55

Graduating Student Seeking First Nursing Position in a Mental Health Setting, 57

Appendix B   Graduating Student Cover Letter, 59

Appendix C   The Interview Guide, 61

Step 1: Preparation, 61
        Attitude, 61
        Plan, 61
Step 2: The Interview, 61
Step 3: Follow-Up, 62

Career Planning and Development as a Student Activity

Welcome to *Building Your Nursing Career*. The rapidly changing world of health care offers nursing students tremendous opportunities, as well as significant challenges. Nursing students now learn in a variety of settings and thus have a firsthand look at nurses who work alone, with other nurses, or in multidisciplinary teams in roles as clinicians, educators, researchers, consultants, or managers. Changes in nursing and the health care system have created an environment in which individuals must become career resilient and self-directed and in which they must take control of their careers and futures. Developing the skills necessary for career resilience is a process that students should engage in as soon as they begin their nursing education.

Career resilience is about flexibility and adaptability. As a career-resilient student nurse, you seek and take advantage of meaningful and career-enhancing experiences both in the classroom and in clinical settings. You develop a growing sense of who you are as a nursing professional and are able to develop incrementally as you move through your educational program. Career-resilient students are dedicated to the idea of continuous learning and stand ready to reinvent themselves to keep pace with change. Moreover, career resilience conforms to the many definitions of nursing professional practice that include autonomy, self-direction, and continual learning.

In your student role, you are exposed to a wide range of clinical settings and learn about many theoretical and technological advances, as well as the current issues in nursing, the health care system, and society as a whole. In the midst of all your discoveries, it is often easy to lose sight of the career goals and aspirations that brought you to nursing. You may need and want help to plan and develop your career so that you orchestrate, rather than merely accumulate, your learning experiences.

How can I plan my career? What are the opportunities today and what will they be in the future? How can I best use my educational experiences to advance my career goals? How can I be employable one or several years from now? Who can help me? These are the questions student nurses are asking. You came to nursing with dreams, goals, and ideas about your future. You need a process to guide you in achieving your maximum potential as a student nurse so that you can actualize your dreams or alter them in response to your growing nursing experience and identification. Career planning and development is a dynamic process that adapts to the changes you will encounter as you build your nursing knowledge and experience.

The purposes of *Building Your Nursing Career* are twofold: (1) to enhance your awareness of career planning and development and its importance today and in the future, and (2) to introduce you to a career planning and development model and a variety of career planning and development activities you can use throughout your nursing career. This guide is intended to provide you with the skills you need to build your career in nursing. We hope you find it informative and useful.

HOW TO USE YOUR STUDENT GUIDE

This guide introduces you to the Donner-Wheeler Career Planning and Development Model (Figure 1-1). This Model is a tool you can use throughout your nursing education to help you develop as a professional and to build your career in a meaningful way. Each phase of the Model (scanning, assessing, visioning, planning, and marketing) is described along with specific activities and exercises to help you develop skill in using the Model at all points in your educational program and later throughout the other stages of your career. You can use the Model to help you develop your clinical learning plan, select courses, determine foci for course assignments, engage in extracurricular activities and, most important, to experience a sense of control over your academic career. Try to encourage your student colleagues to work together as you engage in the career planning and development process. As peers you can offer each other support, feedback, and affirmation as you create your careers.

Your first step should be to read about each phase of the Model—what it is, why it is important, and how to use it. Then turn to the activities at the end of each phase and complete the questions. Each activity will help you tailor the career-building process to your own situation. As you become comfortable with the process, you will be able to move back and forth with ease among the five phases as you gather new experiences, skills, and knowledge.

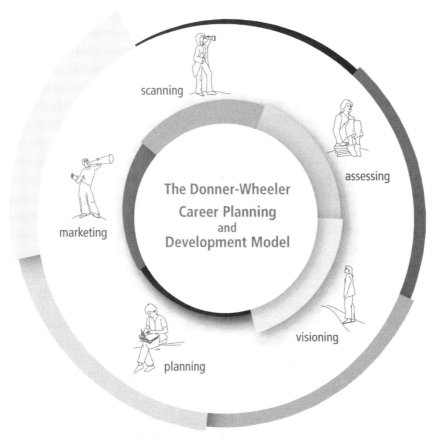

Figure **1-1.** Donner-Wheeler Career Planning and Development Model.

This guide is directed primarily to undergraduate students who are entering nursing for the first time. However, the process and exercises provided are relevant to all nursing program and nursing education experiences. If you want to learn more about the Model and the career planning and development process, you can read *Taking Control of Your Nursing Career*, second edition (2004). That text is directed to nurses at all stages of their career and will be an informative and helpful resource for you as you continue in your nursing career.

CAREER PLANNING AND DEVELOPMENT

A career is described as one's chosen profession, path, or course of life work. Students often think that their nursing career starts at the completion of their education program and that active involvement in career planning becomes important only as they near graduation. In fact, you have chosen a path; your career has already started! You made an important life decision and began your professional career in nursing the day you registered for nursing. The career planning and development model presented in this guide provides you with a process by which you can develop your unique career goals and influence your educational activities to help you succeed in achieving your goals—regardless of where you are in your nursing program.

WHY CAREER PLANNING AND DEVELOPMENT IS IMPORTANT FOR NURSING STUDENTS

Nursing students are at various stages of entering a health care system that offers incredibly diverse opportunities for professional practice. Students describe feeling both excited and anxious when faced with the range of possibilities open to them—both in clinical placement settings and in their future nursing practice. As John, a fourth-year nursing student, observed:

> I am currently completing a very important phase of my life by graduating. At the same time, I will be entering one of the most exciting phases by officially starting a career in nursing. What I am realizing is that I am the only one responsible for my career. Opportunities will not simply fall into my hands; rather, I need to take charge and control my professional future through career planning. I know there are lots of jobs out there; I want to make sure I accept a job that is right for me and fits with my career plans.

Although at a different level in her nursing education program, Leah, a second-year student, described similar feelings:

> I've just finished my second year and I feel like I now have only 2 years left to make sure I get all of the experience I can to be marketable when I graduate. I'm not sure what my goals are or how I can "work the system" to make sure I get what I need.

The career planning process can serve as a guide to help students to achieve a sense of control and focus related to their educational activities and to prepare for future employment. The career planning and development process helps students to answer the following questions:

- Where have I been (before nursing school and over the course of my program)?
- Where am I now? What am I learning and where are my interests?
- Where would I like to go? What are my hopes for my next step in my education and for my future practice?
- How will I get there? How can I plan my courses and make the best of my clinical placements so that I can move toward my goals?

The answers to these questions will be quite different for students at varying stages in their education:

> Over the course of his nursing education, John (the fourth-year student) accumulated a solid foundation of clinical experiences and professional courses. As a result, his responses to the questions will reflect a wide range of nursing-related knowledge and experience.
>
> Leah, the second-year student, may not have the same breadth of clinical experience and range of course work as John, but she can build on her beginning foundation in nursing, her life experiences, and her hopes and dreams for her professional education. Reflecting on these questions can help Leah acknowledge all that she has brought to the profession and how her nursing education can serve to guide her future plans.

Regardless of where you are in your education program, the career planning process involves thought, insight, and dedicated time. Although many resources are available for you to use in planning your career, the one most important to your career development is you! The career planning and development process is really about developing a life skill—one that you can apply not only in your educational and professional endeavours but also in your personal life.

THE DONNER-WHEELER CAREER PLANNING AND DEVELOPMENT MODEL

Career development is not a one-time activity, nor do you need to follow a step-by-step process. Once you have worked through the Model, you can move back and forth among the phases, adding and changing the content of your insights, information, and plans to reflect your developing nursing practice. The Model allows you to track your progress in your professional growth in nursing and to plan for your upcoming learning activities. In your educational program you have built-in cues about when to "check in" with your career development. End-of-terms, evaluation times, and the development of learning plans signal transition times that you can use to guide and build on your work with the career model. The career development process will prompt you to do the following:

1. Understand and use the environment around you to help you develop your nursing practice.
2. Assess your growing strengths and limitations and validate that assessment.
3. Envision what your nursing career can be.
4. Develop a plan for using your educational activities in a way that will help you to move toward your career vision.
5. Market yourself to achieve your career goals.

Career development helps you to stay focused and challenged so that you can create learning opportunities related to your goals or find meaning in experiences that, at face value, do not seem relevant or responsive to your immediate learning needs. The five phases of the Model include the following items listed in the box below.

The Donner-Wheeler Career Planning and Development Model

Phase One: Scanning Your Environment
What are the current realities/future trends?

Phase Two: Completing Your Self-Assessment and Reality Check
Who am I?
How do others see me?

Phase Three: Creating Your Career Vision
What do I really want to be doing?

Phase Four: Developing Your Strategic Career Plan
How can I achieve my career goals?

Phase Five: Marketing Yourself
How can I best market myself?

Planning Your Career

You are now ready to learn to use the Donner-Wheeler Career Planning and Development Model (the Model). This chapter provides you with the details of each of the Model's five phases, along with examples from student lives and experiences. We have included activities to help you apply the Model to your particular educational level and personal and professional goals. Take time to review each phase carefully, and then proceed with the exercises. Remember, this is not a one-time activity but something you will want and need to come back to as your environment, experience, and interests change.

PHASE ONE: SCANNING YOUR ENVIRONMENT

What Is Scanning?

Scanning the environment involves simply looking around you with the goal of identifying how your immediate and surrounding environment can help you develop and achieve your career goals. You have already been introduced to the process of scanning the environment as a nursing student. As you learn to plan and deliver nursing care, you also learn to observe your client's environment and the variables that influence the client's health status (e.g., resources, social factors, economic realities). Your nursing curriculum also offers you structured opportunities, usually in classes and seminars, to learn about important elements of an environmental scan, such as current issues in nursing, health care, work design, and society at large.

Scanning the environment and then identifying your own strengths and interests will give you the information you need to help you identify possibilities for your current and future nursing practice experiences, professional skill development, and course selection. It helps you to answer the following questions:

- What opportunities are available?
- What do I need to be aware of as I think about my career?
- What and who are my resources?

The breadth of your environmental scan may vary depending on where you are in your nursing program. In the early years of your program, you may find it most helpful to concentrate your scan on your school, curriculum requirements, clinical placement settings, and the information available through these resources. In the first and second years of your program, the primary focus of your scan is likely to be on discovering and using the school environment to your best advantage. As you advance, you will be looking toward preparing for graduation and entry to practice. Your preparation will rely on greater knowledge of what is happening outside your immediate learning environment. Extending your scan to include learning about health care and nursing-specific issues and trends locally, statewide/provincially, nationally, and even internationally will be an important next step.

Students are at a definite advantage when doing environmental scans. You have ready access to this information from your course work, faculty members, and clinical agencies. Using the scan to help you with your career planning is just another way to apply your learning. You are already ahead of the game!

Why Is Scanning Important?

Scanning helps you to discover opportunities within your nursing program as well as current and future employment opportunities. It can help you make the best of your learning experiences and identify both short-term and long-term learning activities in keeping with your goals and interests. Without continuous scanning, it is difficult to focus your skill development to your best advantage, difficult to know the best direction in which to head, and even more difficult to influence your learning activities and professional development.

How and When Do You Scan?

The simple answer is—continuously! You can scan throughout your educational program to learn what is happening now and what may happen in the future. Sources of information include the following:

- Course readings
- Discussions with faculty and preceptors
- Professional and popular journals, print, and other forms of news media
- The Internet
- Observations
- Friends and colleagues
- Everyday experiences

Reading, talking, and listening are the means you will use to make sense of the information you collect. As students, you have the added benefit of a number of faculty, preceptors, and student colleagues who are "at your fingertips" to help you both interpret and use the information you will collect in your scan. Once you have gathered all the information, it is helpful to organize it into school, local, national, and global categories. You can add information to these categories at any time.

You should think of your scan as a work in progress—something you continually update and revise to reflect your growing knowledge and understanding of the nursing world. Students often complete a scan with the broad goal of determining areas of focus for their clinical placement experiences and course selection. Hence, they may concentrate their scan on local and school-related trends and issues. Students in the latter years of the program find that extending their focus to provincial/state and national levels gives them information they need to plan for entry to practice. Whatever your focus, try to make scanning an integral part of your everyday academic and personal life.

> Laura, a third-year nursing student, first used the environmental scan to help her look at an upcoming clinical placement. In the winter term she will be going to a community health setting. She is interested in using her scan to help develop a clear focus for her learning plan for the coming term—one that will allow her to concentrate on overall learning goals in addition to the serendipitous learning that would naturally occur in a new placement setting.
>
> Laura began her scan by obtaining the course readings related to the community health course. A brief look at the readings gave her an idea of current issues and trends in community health nursing, both nationally and locally. She then met with two faculty members with expertise in community health nursing. Discussions regarding the nature of community health nursing, nursing roles in community health, and local issues and trends helped her to get a sense of what she could anticipate in her winter placement. Faculty were also able to direct her to informative community health nursing journals. Checking the newspaper and the Internet also provided information relevant to community health care in general.
>
> Finally, Laura phoned her contact person at the community placement setting and asked what she could do to prepare for her placement. With all of this information in hand, she decided on two broad learning goals: (1) developing knowledge and skill in community-based program planning and evaluation, and (2) strengthening her skill in working within a family-centred care model in the community context. Her self-assessment would then help her to specify learning objectives related to these goals.

Now that you understand what scanning is and how to use it, try Activity 1.

Activity 1: Scanning Your Environment

> The trends and issues you identify in your scan can help you to make decisions about potential opportunities within your classroom and clinical environments. The following is a guide you can use to help you with your scan. Consider the areas of school, local, and national. If you feel ready to extend your scan to the global level, then include that category as well.
>
> For each of the categories (school, local, national, global), consider issues related to society, to health in general, and to nursing. Insert those trends and issues you observe to be important at this time. To help you as you fill in your scan, we have provided you with some questions to consider with a sampling of possible answers. Your list of questions and answers will likely grow over time.
>
> Remember that you will need to review and revise your scan on a regular basis. The end of each term can be a cue to update your scan.

School

- What are some of the opportunities/realities of your school setting?

    Components of the nursing curriculum, required courses, course electives, placement opportunities, faculty resources/mentors, student association representatives, interdisciplinary courses.

Local

- What are some of the important social and health issues in your local area?

    Changing demographics of the client population, shift in care to the community, increasing caregiver burden, patient and workplace safety, environment.

- What are the important nursing issues in your local area?

    Shortage/surplus of nurses, demographics (e.g., aging) of nurses, changing practice settings, changing roles in the practice setting.

National

- What are the significant health and social trends?

    Controlling health care costs, decreasing lengths of hospital stays, community-based care, infant mortality, increased use of technology.

- What are the issues affecting nurses?

    Shortage of nurses, education specialization, quality of worklife.

Global

- What health/social issues seem to be worldwide phenomena?

    Infectious diseases, ethical issues, allocation of resources, gap between rich and poor, social determinants of health.

- What nursing issues seem to be global in scope?

    Recruitment and retention, regulation, quality of worklife, changing practice.

Scanning Your Environment

School		
Curriculum/Courses	Placement Opportunities	Faculty Resources

Local Trends and Issues		
Society	Health Care	Nursing

National Trends and Issues		
Society	Health Care	Nursing

Global Trends and Issues		
Society	Health Care	Nursing

What Have You Accomplished?

Completing an initial environmental scan has given you some valuable information about what is available in your school, the issues nurses currently face, and the type of opportunities available for your current clinical experiences and future nursing practice. This information helps you to see what is possible and realistic so you can choose a focus and make the best of your learning experiences.

What Is Your Next Step?

You now have a better understanding of the nursing and health care world. The next step is getting a sense of how your interests, values, and abilities fit with what is available. This process is called self-assessment. After completing the self-assessment, you should do a reality check of it with others.

PHASE TWO: COMPLETING YOUR SELF-ASSESSMENT AND REALITY CHECK

What Is Self-Assessment?

Your self-assessment helps you to identify your values, experiences, knowledge, strengths, and limitations and then link them with your environmental scan to plan the next educational steps you wish to take. When you scanned the environment, you focused on noticing what surrounds you and on building an understanding of how that influences your present and future development. The self-assessment focuses on *you*. It can assist you in recognizing all the attributes that make you who you are, what areas you would like to focus on for further development, and what you have to offer. Your self-assessment also provides you with the opportunity to think about how your personal life goals influence, and are influenced by, your career development and your career choices. Completing your self-assessment and reality check will allow you to give honest and accurate answers to two questions: (1) Who am I?, and (2) How do others see me? When you put your self-assessment together with the results of your environmental scan, your replies will enable you to complete the last three phases of the career planning and development process: creating your career vision, developing your strategic career plan, and marketing yourself to implement your plan.

Why Is Assessing Yourself Important?

As a student nurse, an awareness of your values, skills, and strengths will provide insight into what you have brought to the profession as a nursing student and what areas you would like to develop further. It forms an important basis for preparing you to make plans and develop the type of career and future that suits you and is what you want.

Some students believe they have no say in planning their educational experiences. It is true that nursing curricula, like those in other professional disciplines, have required courses and learning activities, and you may not have a choice about whether to take those courses. However, you can choose how to interpret and use these courses to meet your unique needs. In addition to the required courses, there is usually a range of elective courses from which you can select according to your interests and preferences. Within both scenarios, your ability to use your learning to meet your professional and personal learning needs (preferably similar) depends on how well you know yourself. Self-knowledge of interests, values, knowledge, skills, strengths, and limitations can help you look at any experience as a meaningful learning opportunity. Sharing your assessment helps others to respond to your unique needs.

In many ways, as a nursing student you have an advantage in this fundamental step of the career planning and development process. Most nursing curricula require that you participate in some form of self-reflection and self-evaluation. The key to success is to find meaning in the doing. Too often, nursing students approach the self-reflective process as an academic exercise rather than as a means of enhancing their own career development. Once you claim the process of reflection as your own, you will be able to capitalize on your identified strengths and life experiences across all dimensions of your educational experiences. Revisiting your self-assessment at the end of each term will allow you to update your knowledge of self, set new learning goals, develop career goals and action plans, and feel confident that you will find, or create, meaning in your future learning experiences.

Beginning the Self-Assessment Process

The first questions are "Who am I?" and "How would you describe yourself?" Answering these questions involves much more than describing what you do or where you are in your educational preparation. Even though you spend a considerable amount of time at school (and, perhaps, at work) to support your academic endeavours, it is important to acknowledge those other components that complete your life, including your personal health, well-being, and development; your family and friends; your community; and your personal life goals.

Although you may be new to nursing, you have had valuable life experiences that have contributed to your current strengths in nursing. For example, think about all the adjectives you could use to detail what makes you unique. Although we are all unique, the challenge lies in being able to articulate that uniqueness. Can you make a list of three characteristics that define your uniqueness? Pick up a pencil and paper and make that list—now! Keep that list and refer to it and revise it from time to time. As a matter of fact, this would be a good time to begin keeping a journal of your thoughts and dreams. Journaling is a powerful tool to help you keep track of where you are headed and all the ideas and plans you have to help you get there. It is your private record of who you are, what is important to you, and how you are changing. Many people have found journaling a valuable resource for "sorting things out."

Who we are includes our beliefs and values, our knowledge and skills, our interests, and our hopes for our future. Beliefs are the way in which we view ourselves and the world around us. Values are a set of beliefs that drive our decisions, actions, behaviours, and relations. Knowledge and skills are the abilities and behaviours we use to produce results, and interests are the activities in which we like to spend most of our time and from which we gain pleasure.

Assessing Your Values

Values are those principles we prize and cherish—those beliefs we hold as extremely important. Values direct our decisions and influence our lives. As you begin to identify your values, consider why you chose nursing as a career and how your experiences to date fit with those values. Ask yourself the following questions:
- What is important to me in my educational and personal life?
- What significant experiences or interests prompted me to consider nursing as a career?
- Who has inspired me in my nursing education? What values did that person convey?
- What can I contribute to nursing?
- What values influence my learning and my development as a nurse?
- Who or what are the significant things in my life that I need to consider at this time?
- What are my priorities—self, partner, family, school, work, community, or other?

> Maria recognized the strong influence her mother had on her choice of nursing as a career. Her mother, who had been a nurse, exemplified warmth, caring, and strength—the qualities Maria associated with nursing. In addition to demonstrating respect for the uniqueness and integrity of each individual, Maria's mother modelled the power of nursing to influence the quality of health care. She accomplished this through individual interactions both with clients and with her nursing colleagues. Her mother's willingness to campaign for those not able to advocate for themselves fostered the value Maria places on the importance of individual efforts in influencing the perceptions and actions of decision makers at all levels of health care.
>
> Maria also had the opportunity to accompany her mother when she volunteered at a senior citizen's home. During these visits Maria directly observed the positive effect her mother and the other nurses had on the residents through their professional presence and individualized approach to care. Long-term exposure to this setting fostered Maria's interest in nursing as a career, with a possible focus on working with older adults. In addition, her teachers, family members, and friends told her she was very good with people and would make a great nurse. Knowing that she had the potential to be a warm, caring, and committed professional and that she was interested in working closely with people helped Maria to decide that nursing was a good career choice.
>
> Maria states, "It's funny. I always knew I wanted to be a nurse, to make a difference in people's lives, but it wasn't until I sat down and really thought about *why* I wanted to be a nurse that I realized what an excellent role model my mom has been and how that modelling has influenced my decision to go into nursing, with a possible focus on geriatric nursing. I can see how I have come to value many of the things my mom does and how these values will help me to be an effective nurse. I was also able to get a first-hand view of how rewarding it can be to care for this client population."

Assessing Your Knowledge and Skills

Recognizing what knowledge and skills you possess—and to what degree you possess them—are crucial outcomes of the self-assessment process. Knowledge develops through a combination of formal learning and experience, whereas skills are acquired abilities. By reviewing your past accomplishments, clinical and classroom evaluations, and nursing program goals, you can begin to identify your strengths and the areas you would like to develop further. Consider the work you have done within your nursing program and in your non-nursing life. Your community and social environments also provide opportunities for increasing knowledge and skills about people and the world in which you live.

As you accumulate classroom and clinical experiences, you will gather current feedback related to your strengths, your progress, and areas to develop from a variety of instructors, peers, and clinical contacts. Remember to seek and value feedback that relates to all of your professional skills, not just your psychomotor skill set. In the past, job requirements tended to relate only to job duties or "hard skills" (e.g., those involved with providing direct nursing care to clients), not to work attitudes, general communication, and interpersonal skills. When you sit down to evaluate your skills, take into account your personality and nature, your attitude, the way you work with others, and your ease of communication. These attributes or "soft skills" are as important as your technical clinical skills and often are highly transferable.

Knowledge and skill gaps or limitations are just as important to acknowledge as your strengths. If you do not recognize these limitations, you may miss important learning opportunities.

You should ask yourself the following questions:

- What knowledge and skills have I developed both personally and professionally?
- What are my strengths?
- What are my limitations?
- What knowledge and skills require further development?

Many of the successes and strengths you have enjoyed in other areas of your life will hold you in good stead in your nursing career. If you are in the first year of your nursing program, start by considering your past accomplishments with a focus on the values, insight, skills, and strengths that you developed as a result of your efforts.

> Dominic identified his involvement on the high school rowing team as an accomplishment. When he focused on the skills he had developed as a result of this experience, he identified strengths in teamwork, an ability to successfully balance academic and extracurricular activities, and effective coaching skills with new team members. Reflecting on his positive experiences with his rowing team also helped Dominic realize how much he values working as part of a team. Each of these skills and insights will be an asset to him in his nursing career.

> Indira was employed as a nanny for three young children during the summer months. She was able to identify her knowledge related to the developmental issues and needs of the preschool and school-aged child, the enjoyment she experienced when working with children, and her strengths in the areas of organization, patience, and perseverance. Indira also noted how her experience as a nanny heightened her awareness of her values related to the importance of family in the lives of children.

After identifying their strengths and skills, students can focus on enhancing them in the context of their nursing experience by asking for specific feedback and seeking experiences to meet their unique learning needs. Awareness of their values can also add insight and clarity to their reflection and evaluation of each learning experience.

Assessing Your Interests

Interests provide another guide in determining your current and future learning goals and in deciding how you would ideally like to meet those goals. They can be grouped into four categories:

- People: Helping, serving, caring for, or selling things to people
- Data: Working with facts, records, or files
- Things: Working with machines, tools, or living things such as plants and animals
- Ideas: Creating insights, theories, or new ways of saying or doing something

What have you liked about your past and current job(s), summer employment, part-time jobs, academic jobs (e.g., research assistant, work-study student), or volunteer activities? What haven't you liked? In what type of environment do you learn and perform at your best? What do you like to do outside of the academic environment and/or your current workplace? What energizes or motivates you? Answering these questions will help you understand and articulate your interests.

Recognizing Your Accomplishments

Accomplishments refer to those specific successes that have marked the highlights of your performance in any of your roles (e.g., student nurse, volunteer, and employee). For example, you may have developed a patient/client teaching package, provided an in-service for the staff at your clinical placement, or received acknowledgment or recognition for your strong communication or leadership skills within your student role. These accomplishments represent those times in your life that you made a difference. They become the added value you will bring to any nursing practice environment.

Data from your self-assessment help you to interpret and structure your learning experiences in a way that is relevant and meaningful to you. The more you learn and reflect on your development as a nurse, the more you can begin to influence your learning experiences.

> A detailed self-assessment was invaluable to Jacob, a fourth-year student in the process of deciding where he would like to complete his final-year clinical placements. Jacob was undecided about whether he should request a medical-surgical setting or a long-term-care setting. In the process of completing his self-assessment, he discovered that he (1) valued the continuity of working with adult clients who experience chronic illness, (2) was interested in working with people over time, (3) had strengths in psychomotor/technical skills and in developing therapeutic relationships with clients who require long-term care, and (4) needed further knowledge in the area of the psychosocial needs of clients experiencing chronic illness.
>
> Jacob created a learning plan that acknowledged his existing strengths and focused on those "hard" and "soft" skills needed to work effectively with chronically ill clients who require long-term care. Through his environmental scan, Jacob had recently identified broad trends and needs related to care of the adult client with a chronic illness and of long-term clients in general. Based on information from his scan and self-assessment, he decided to request an adult inpatient medical placement in the first term and an outpatient clinic targeting adult clients at various phases in their chronic illness for his final term.

In most nursing education programs, students are required to complete their clinical placements in organizations that provide experiences congruent with the general goals of the curriculum. Knowing the skills necessary to achieve expertise in your area of interest can help you to make the best of any clinical placement experience, even if the placement is not of your choosing. A comprehensive scan of the environment, together with data from your self-assessment, will provide you with the information you need to capitalize on available learning opportunities.

In the previous example, Jacob's awareness of his values, interests, knowledge, and areas for further development provided direction for his professional educational goals that he could use to guide his learning in any setting. By formulating a learning plan focused on skill development for the care of long-term clients, he could shape his clinical learning experience to enhance his skills related to work with clients experiencing chronic illness, even if his clinical placement was primarily acute care. Alternatively, he could focus on those skills that are transferable between acute care and chronic care.

Another fourth-year nursing student describes how information from the self-assessment process helped him evaluate different clinical experiences:

> Throughout my 4 years I would imagine "putting on the hat" of a specialty of nursing that had caught my attention. I would gather information about this particular area through reading, talking to nurses, and attending conferences. I was assessing the match between my interests and talents (gathered through the self-assessment) and the nursing specialty that interested me at that time.

Through ongoing self-assessment, this student recognized his strength in interpersonal communication, specifically in the establishment of therapeutic, goal-directed relationships with individual clients. He also valued the mutuality of the nurse-client relationship. This self-knowledge helped him to evaluate the "fit" between an area of nursing practice and a unique professional skill:

> I became interested in nursing informatics. I went to conferences, read books, and talked to some nurses in the informatics area. I imagined the work I would be doing and explored what I would need to get involved. In the end, it didn't feel right to me. I liked computers and had a good idea of their potential in the nursing profession, but I wanted to work more with people and ideas—not with machines, data, and policy. My interest in informatics as a career focus faded and was replaced by a new interest—a new "hat" that was more congruent with my values and strengths.

A third-year student found that by keeping her values at the centre of her clinical placement planning, she was able to develop skills and expertise that would be an asset in any setting:

> My mother had to spend a fair amount of time in the hospital, and I was so appreciative of the nurses who took the time to talk to us and help us, as her family, to understand what was happening and how we could help her. I don't know what specialty I want to work in, but I do know that I want to practice family-centred care, and I want to know how to communicate not only with patients, but with families. Knowing this, I make a point to have the development of skills in family-centred care and communication as my learning goal for each placement. If I let my instructor and the other nurses on the unit know about my interest in these areas, they can assign me to patients who will offer the opportunity to work on these skills. I find it difficult to be on units in which there is no visiting during the day and there is little time to talk to patients; I don't think I could work on a unit like that.

Now you are ready to complete your self-assessment in Activity 2.

Activity 2: Completing Your Self-Assessment

> The following are some preliminary questions that can help you understand who you are and what is important to you. Your answers will give you the words to describe your unique self, what you like to do, and what you have to offer. As you start to document your answers, you can begin to write your own story. Your story should include all the important personal and professional events in your life and how they relate to one another.

1. Values: What Are My Priorities?

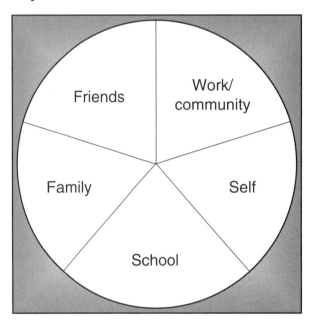

Mark the percentage of time you spend daily in each section of the circle. Now ask yourself the following questions:

- What is most important to me in my current nursing education experiences?

    (Examples: Access to professional role models, a good "fit" between coursework and clinical experiences, opportunity to spend time with clients, program's responsiveness to current health care realities)

- What is important to me as a nursing student and in my personal life?

    (Examples: Relationships, fairness, honesty, balance, knowing my strengths and my limitations)

- Who or what are the significant things in my life that I need to consider at this time?

    (Examples: Spending time with family, spouse/partner, boyfriend/girlfriend; part-time job)

2. Knowledge and Skills

- What knowledge and skills have I developed both personally and professionally in my nursing program and outside of my nursing educational experiences?

    (Examples: Self-directed learning, resourcefulness, flexibility, therapeutic communication [empathy, support, listening])

2. Knowledge and Skills—cont'd

- What new knowledge and skills have I acquired since my last self-assessment?

    (Examples: Technical skills in medical-surgical areas such as IV monitoring, complex dressings, medication administration; leadership skills in giving report and in participating in interdisciplinary case meetings)

- What are my strengths?

    (Examples: Communication skills, specifically empathy, open-ended questions, establishing positive rapport; organizational skills; responsibility and accountability in practice; resourcefulness, eagerness, enthusiasm)

- What are my limitations?

    (Examples: Limited knowledge base regarding psychosocial care of the client with a chronic illness, confidence in challenging physicians when I need to advocate for a client, documentation skills)

- What knowledge and skills would I like to develop in my current or next term?

    (Examples: Theory related to coping with chronic illness, family-centred care theory in a community-care context, effective client teaching, legal/ethical issues related to outpatient care)

3. Interests

- What have I liked about my clinical placement experience(s)?

    (Examples: Developing therapeutic relationships with clients, professional role modelling, positive teamwork)

- What clinical experience has been most exciting for me?

    (Examples: Rehabilitation in which I was able to spend time getting to know clients; a slower pace in which I felt I had more control and independence in how I organized my care; time to consult and collaborate with other nurses)

- What courses have been of most interest to me?

    (Examples: Nursing concepts, psychology, transcultural nursing, community nursing)

3. Interests—cont'd

- What placements and courses have I not liked?

    (Examples: I liked them all because I learn something in each one. The ones that were very fast-paced and "technical" were not as rewarding to me, although I learned a lot about organization and "hands on" skills)

- What energizes or motivates me?

    (Examples: Positive feedback from faculty, feedback from clients that I do make a difference, meeting my own goals, relaxation with family and friends, a good workout)

- In what type of learning environment (class/clinical) do I perform my best?

    (Examples: Any environment in which there is interaction and a lot of discussion and in which I feel that what I have to say or contribute is important)

- What do I like to do outside of my academic environment?

    (Examples: Spend time outdoors, read, spend time with the people I care about, exercise)

- What is important to me in my physical environment?

    (Examples: Being located in a warm climate, being located in a rural/urban setting, being located close to my friends and family, relocating to establish myself apart from familiar places and people)

4. Accomplishments

- What have been my most significant accomplishments in my nursing education to date? Outside of my education?

    (Examples: Invited to join my school's honour society; elected as student representative on school council; told by my employer that I was an excellent "trainer" for new staff; told by my preceptor that I have very good leadership skills for my level; have a lot of good friends and am a good friend to others)

- Can I describe those times in my life when I made a difference?

    (Examples: When I had my placement at the rehabilitation unit, I organized a game show for the residents and staff. The staff said they had not seen the residents have so much fun in a long time.)

Your Reality Check

A reality check is about seeking feedback regarding your strengths and limitations. The reality check can help you broaden your view of yourself, because others often see you differently from how you see yourself. Once you have completed your self-assessment and have answered the question "Who am I?," it is important to validate your answers by doing a reality check. It will provide information that will help you answer the next critical question: "How do others see me?"

Students often find that the reality check provides an opportunity to be informed or reminded of strengths and attributes that they do not recognize in themselves. Keep in mind that your social, family, and community networks are also important sources of feedback about your knowledge, skills, strengths, and limitations. Armed with your regular formal evaluations from faculty, peers, and nursing contacts, as well as with your expanding nursing experience and your initial assessment of your accomplishments as you enter nursing, you have what you need to update your self-assessment on an ongoing basis.

Why Is a Reality Check Crucial?

Getting feedback affirms where we shine and at times identifies knowledge or skill gaps that need to be filled. As a student, you receive and respond to feedback on a continual basis. A good deal of the feedback you receive is tied to specific course or curriculum goals. Although this feedback is of value in determining and reinforcing your expanding professional strengths and areas for further development, it may not address the areas of self-assessment that you would like confirmed or viewed from another perspective. Therefore be prepared to request specific feedback related to your self-assessment if your sources of course and program feedback do not address all your unique needs.

How Do You Do a Reality Check?

Start with those individuals you trust—family, student peers, and others who know you well. Then consider getting feedback from an individual whom you know, but not that well (perhaps a preceptor, or another nurse in your clinical placement area), and ask him or her the same questions. You can also refer to your clinical placement evaluations and course feedback. Individuals often find that the reality check provides an opportunity to be informed or reminded of strengths and attributes that they do not recognize in themselves. The reality check component of the self-assessment process can strengthen your confidence in communicating your skills and uniqueness to colleagues, potential employers, and other professionals. For example, during the reality check step, a third-year nursing student became aware of a strength she had not previously identified:

> I took my self-assessment to a faculty member whom I really like and respect. She confirmed the strengths that I had identified and, to my surprise, added something that I never would have considered. She said my sense of humour was excellent and allowed me to establish rapport with clients in a very gentle and non-threatening manner. Now when I care for clients, I am conscious of my use of humour and can see that it is unique and can be therapeutic.

Now you are ready to do your reality check. Complete Activity 3.

Activity 3: Reality Check

> Review your self-assessment and reread your accomplishments. Then ask yourself the following questions.

- What feedback have I received from faculty members, preceptors, clients, student colleagues, friends, and family regarding my achievements?

- What did they identify as my strengths and limitations?

- What three adjectives would they (or did they) use to describe me, both within and outside the academic/clinical environment or workplace? Why?

- How did my assessment of my accomplishments compare with others' assessments?

- What has changed since my last reality check?

Piece together all the data and create a written summary of your strengths and challenges. With an accurate sense of who you are and how others see you, you will be ready to explore a range of opportunities and determine how you can focus your next learning experience.

What Have You Accomplished?

The self-assessment process has allowed you to think about what is important to you, what you do well, and what you need to learn and develop further. You have also received confirmation from others that you are on track. Checking back to your environmental scan, you can get a sense of the fit and gaps between your strengths and limitations and the opportunities "out there"—both for learning and for your future practice.

What Is Your Next Step?

Dreaming! No doubt your self-assessment has given you better insight about your values, interests, and strengths as they relate to your nursing career. Now you can give yourself the freedom to dream about what those attributes will look like in the future. Close your eyes, put your feet up, and picture yourself as a nurse doing exactly what you want to do and doing it well.

PHASE THREE: CREATING YOUR CAREER VISION

What Is a Career Vision?

Your career vision is the link between who you are and what you can become. Once you have determined a realistic and comprehensive picture of your own values, beliefs, knowledge, and skills, and have looked at those in the context of your environmental scan, you are ready to think about how you can orchestrate your educational experiences to help you meet your career options. Start by asking yourself the following questions:

- What type of nurse do I hope to be?
- Where do I see myself going?

Why Should I Have a Career Vision?

Having a career vision is perhaps the most forceful motivator for using your clinical and classroom experiences, and your summer and part-time work opportunities, to the fullest. Your vision can help you focus on how you can make the best of your learning opportunities rather than just reacting to events as they occur. Creating a career vision answers the question, "What do I want?" With an idea of what you would like your career to look like, you can approach any course or clinical placement with a sense of how it may help you get where you want to go. With each new encounter you have with the world of nursing, your career vision may alter or may perhaps change all together. Therefore you should continually ask yourself, "Am I still feeling the way I felt about nursing when I entered my nursing program?" You can use your journal to continue to explore and reflect on this question as you move along in your nursing program and your nursing career.

Student nurses are often uncertain about how they can design their career futures while still in their education program. Just as with courses, it is unlikely that individual students have their choice of where they will have their clinical experiences. Nor can they select all of their courses to suit their current interests. However, students can approach any clinical setting, classroom environment, or work or volunteer experience with focused goals that are congruent with their self-assessment and career vision. These personal learning goals may be an added dimension to the learning that is structured through the curriculum. Often it is in clinical practice settings that are seemingly unrelated to their career visions that students can be the most creative and active in shaping their learning. Many students find that when they optimize opportunities, as opposed to resisting the unknown, they end up discovering more choices than they had ever considered.

> Jalynn, a second-year student with a career goal of maternal-child nursing was placed in a mental health setting. She expressed concern that she would need to put her maternal-child nursing focus "on hold" during this placement experience. In spite of a seeming lack of fit between her career goal and the area of mental health, she shared her career goal with both her clinical instructor and her preceptor. She was reminded by both that she could focus her learning goals on communication skills and work with any pregnant women admitted to her placement setting. At the end of term Jalynn evaluated her mental health experience as a most valuable learning experience in terms of refining her therapeutic communication skills with both short-term and long-term clients.

How to Create Your Own Career Vision

Creating a career vision involves *affirmation* (composing a statement of what you want to create in your life), *visualization* (forming a picture or image of what you want to create), and *germination* (being committed to a vision you believe will occur). It begins with taking time to do some active daydreaming about an ideal day in your future. Your career vision will be as individual as you are. To create it, you will need to ask yourself some important questions and give yourself permission to let go of what you previously thought possible.

Two general questions will guide you in this process. The question "Where would I like to go?" helps you to get started—rather like a warm-up or brainstorming session. No answer is wrong. The question "What is my ideal vision for my career?" provides more focus as you begin to create your career vision. Formulate your career vision in the present tense, as if it were occurring right now, and formulate it in as much descriptive detail as possible.

> Peter, a second-year nursing student, had just completed his final clinical placement of the year in an adult medical surgical unit. Data from his most recent self-assessment and reality check helped him to determine that he enjoyed and was effective in working with families who were experiencing the hospitalization of a family member with a life-threatening illness. He found that in his last placement he enjoyed working with younger patients, especially an adolescent with a recent diagnosis of cancer. He was able to work with the adolescent and her family for a few weeks and received feedback that he made a positive difference in the hospital experience of this family.
>
> **Career Vision:** I am an expert advanced practice nurse on an active paediatric oncology unit. I feel confident in working with children and families who are experiencing cancer and in serving as a resource and clinical expert for my nursing colleagues.
>
> Although Peter was aware that his ultimate career vision may change as he encounters new areas of professional practice, he developed a vision that reflected where he was at the present.

A third-year student created a career vision statement that reflected her progressive interest in community health nursing:

> In one of my first-year nursing courses, a nurse who worked solely with the homeless population in our city spoke to the class about her nursing experiences. I was hooked! I decided right then that I wanted my nursing practice to centre on caring for homeless clients. I created my career vision and have used my clinical and course

experiences to help me prepare to achieve my goals. Although my vision changes slightly as I learn more about myself, nursing, and the health care system, the essence of my vision has remained fairly constant.

Career Vision: I am an expert community-based nurse with recognized expertise in the needs and care of individuals and groups who live on the streets of large urban centres. I lobby on both local and national levels and serve as a resource to my nursing colleagues, health care policy makers, and the media.

Your career vision does not need to be specific to a specialty area of nursing (e.g., paediatrics, emergency, ICU). Your vision can articulate the type of professional you wish to be. For example, a first-year student developed the following career vision:

Career Vision: I am an expert nurse who is recognized for my extensive knowledge base, my exceptional interpersonal skills, my clinical excellence, and my commitment to collaborative practice.

Lydia, a fourth-year student, looked to her clinical placement experiences as a means to explore a number of career options. Her career vision reflected her desire to be an entrepreneur in her yet undecided clinical specialty:

Career Vision: I am an independent nursing practitioner with specific research and practice expertise working in a consulting role. I work with individual clients and organizations to establish and evaluate programs in my area of clinical expertise. I am recognized for my knowledge, skill, and ability to work effectively and efficiently to produce a relevant "product" of excellent quality.

Whether your career vision involves a clinical specialty, a professional image, or both, it can serve as a motivating guide as you progress toward your dream.

Now you are ready to develop your career vision. Do Activity 4.

Activity 4: Creating Your Career Vision

> When you start, your vision doesn't need to be too realistic; that comes later in the process when you set your career goals. Don't worry about your vision being too big, too vague, or too impossible. It should be grand and inspiring; if it is an important dream, it may even be a little scary. Ask yourself the following questions.

- What do I want? What am I seeking?

- What would my ideal day look like? What am I doing, where am I doing it, and who is there with me?

- Is someone currently doing the type of work I would like to do? Describe the characteristics of that work.

- What stands in the way of my doing what I really want to do? Which of these barriers are really insurmountable?

- What environmental constraints must I consider when planning to do what I really want to do?

- What environmental supports/resources would facilitate my progress toward my career vision?

What Have You Accomplished?

You have put your dream into words. Your dream may change over the course of your educational program, or it may stay with you until your graduation. Either way, your dream can help you create and use your future learning activities. Your dream is your guide.

What Is Your Next Step?

Action! The next step of the career planning process guides you in making plans to use your educational program to help you determine what you need to learn to move toward your career vision. You know what is around you, you know yourself, and you have your dream. Go for it!

PHASE FOUR: DEVELOPING YOUR STRATEGIC CAREER PLAN

What Are Career Plans?

Career plans are like the learning plans you may be asked to develop throughout your academic career. In fact, as you advance in your education, your learning plan should be your career plan. Whether you are working on your learning plan and your career plan as one, or separately, your career plan will guide you to be able to work in partnership with your educational supports and resources to achieve your career goals.

A strategic career plan is a blueprint for action. Now you are ready to specify the goals, activities, timelines, and resources you need to help you achieve your career vision. In this part of the process, you start to put on paper the specific strategies you will use to take charge of your future. The strategic career plan is always a "work in progress"—the object of continual evaluation. As a student you will be constantly scanning your environment, assessing yourself, receiving feedback from others, and evaluating and reevaluating your goals and your plans for reaching them.

Why Should I Develop a Career Plan?

Having a strategic plan helps you take advantage of each planned or unanticipated learning experience. Whatever your career vision, a plan will allow you to recognize unexpected or "accidental" learning experiences as opportunities and, ultimately, to take control of a rewarding career.

The key to a good plan is to ensure that it is both uniquely yours and easily converted into action within your educational experience. It must be derived from your career vision and outline specific actions that you can take to achieve clearly defined goals. Having a strategic career plan helps you make the career goals related to your career vision action-oriented. You may have more than one strategic career plan at the same time. As stated by one student:

> In such turbulent times, I feel that I must have several back-up plans ready to go at once. I keep my career vision fairly broad because I must be ready to shift my specific career goals or options at the drop of a hat. This flexibility and multiple career options allow me to sleep at night, knowing that if I don't get a particular job, I have lots of other possibilities that are still in keeping with my career vision.

How Should I Plan?

A strategic career plan includes identification of the following:

- Goals
- Action steps
- Resources
- Timelines
- Indicators of success

Document your plan—in writing! The exercise of "writing it down" forces you to include each of the critical components and makes it easier for you to continually review, refine, evaluate, and reevaluate both your goals and your progress. It also helps you make a commitment to yourself—to work on making your plan become reality.

Set Goals

Once you have created your career vision, you need to set short-term and long-term career goals or your vision will remain forever only a dream. Choosing and setting goals means that you are serious about taking charge of your learning. When choosing your career goals, always ask yourself, "What do I hope to achieve by pursuing this goal?" Remember to keep the goals specific, time framed, reachable, and relevant. Will anyone who reads them understand what you are trying to accomplish? Do you have actual target dates for achievement? Are your goals realistic enough to be attainable? Are the goals in tune with your future needs?

Career goals should be realistic (I can do it), desirable (I want to do it), and motivating (I will work to make it happen). Remember that you will reevaluate and alter your career goals as you move toward your career vision, or you may perhaps change your vision as you encounter new experiences in your educational program. Even if you change your vision, you can build on the activities and resources you have used in meeting previous goals.

To begin a strategic career plan, Peter, the second-year student with a career vision of being an advanced practice nurse in paediatric oncology, developed the following goals:

Career Vision: I am an expert advanced practice nurse on an active paediatric oncology unit. I feel confident in working with children and families who are experiencing cancer and in serving as a resource and clinical expert for my nursing colleagues.

Short-Term Goals:
1. Secure clinical placement experiences for third and fourth year that will help me develop skills in this area of practice.
2. Find a mentor in the School of Nursing.
3. Network with other nurses in paediatric oncology.

Long-Term Goal: Get a staff nurse position on a paediatric oncology unit on graduation.

Specify the Action Steps

Once you have determined your goals, use specific action steps to further break down goals into discrete and concrete activities. Action steps complete the sentence, "In order to achieve this goal, I will...."

Peter chose the following action steps to help him achieve his short-term goals:
1. Through my environmental scan, identify overall professional skills and specific clinical skills that are most important to work and function competently in paediatric oncology.
2. Update my self-assessment with these skills in mind.
3. Meet with the clinical placement coordinator to discuss placement experiences for third and fourth year that will help me to develop skills in this area.
4. Talk to up to three faculty people who could possibly be mentors.
5. Find the names of senior students who have worked with children with a diagnosis of cancer.

Identify Resources

Having identified specific action steps to take, you are now ready to look at the resources you may need to achieve your goal. The process of developing a plan requires you to think about who and what will help you implement your plan. Making a thoughtful inventory of your available and potential resources is the first step you should take to begin to implement the action steps associated with each of your goals.

> To achieve his goals, Peter identified as resources the school clinical placement coordinator, faculty members with an interest in paediatrics and/or oncology, the nursing student association representative in his school of nursing, the student interest group of the professional nursing organization, his clinical advisor, and his preceptor from his last clinical placement.

Once you have determined the resources you will require, you will be ready to set timelines to accomplish your action steps.

Establish Timelines

If your goal is personally motivating and your plan is realistic and concrete, assigning timelines ensures that you allocate your resources in an efficient and ultimately rewarding way. Timelines should be suited to your particular needs and fit your personal priorities. In the previous example, Peter realized he would need to achieve most of his action plans before the end of the school term. He gave himself 4 weeks to achieve all of his action plans, and he scheduled one to two specific action steps per week.

Timelines can be modified, but including them at the outset is critical to developing an effective career plan.

Identify the Indicators of Success

How will you know that your plan is working? If you have documented your plan, including specific action steps, required resources, and timelines, you have a good start at identifying indicators of success. Think about what you are hoping to accomplish with your plan. For Peter, the indicators of success included having a list of both "hard" and "soft" skills necessary to be a competent paediatric oncology nurse, revising his self-assessment, meeting with the placement coordinator and the student nursing association representative, finding out when the next professional association student interest group meeting would be held, and making appointments with the three faculty members who were active in paediatrics and oncology.

As you design your own plan, think about what success would look like for you. Career plans should be dynamic, responsive to personal circumstances, and professionally stimulating. You should be ready to adjust your plan as aspects of your self-assessment change, as your continually updated environmental scan indicates that significant changes have occurred around you, and as you move forward in your education.

Now you are ready to develop your own strategic career plan. Complete Activity 5.

Activity 5: Developing Your Strategic Career Plan

A well-developed strategic plan not only helps you realize your career vision but also enables you to recognize and take advantage of other career opportunities as they occur.

- Start by putting your written career vision right in front of you.
- Identify your short-term and long-term career goals.
- Complete the following strategic career plan outline.

Strategic Career Plan

Career Vision:

Career Goals:

Action Steps	Resources	When to Accomplish	How Will I Know I Have Succeeded?

Thinking of Graduate Studies?

Pursuing graduate studies may have been your intent from the beginning of your nursing education, or it may be a more recent decision arising from your career vision.

As with any other career decision, you have some important decisions to make. Many students ask the following questions:

- How do I choose the right graduate program?
- How do I sort out the benefits of one program or university compared to another?
- What types of questions should I be asking?
- What can I be doing in my undergraduate program to position me for success in both the application process and program of study?

You can use your strategic career plan to help you answer these important questions. You can integrate this into your existing career planning work (that is, into every phase), or you might actually do a parallel career planning exercise devoted specifically to the pursuit of graduate studies. Either way, you can begin by expanding your environmental scan to include the nature and role of graduate programs in nursing and/or related disciplines. Gather information related to the types of available programs and how they advance the careers of nurses in your area of interest. You can also learn about general graduate education entry requirements—those usually required regardless of the university or program. With the information from your scan in mind, return to your self-assessment with a focus on identifying gaps and strengths most relevant to this career planning strategy. For example, because grades and grade point averages or class standing are almost always a key issue in graduate applications, review your grades and, if necessary, consider how you can ensure that you meet the generally accepted requirements.

The next step in the development of your strategic career plan for graduate studies can focus on gathering information related to the types of programs offered, faculty resources, flexibility of programs with respect to full-time and part-time study options, access to on-line courses, and timelines for degree completion and career opportunities during and at completion of the program. Remember to ask for the philosophy and mission statement of the program so you can determine if the stated values and beliefs about teaching and learning are a good fit with the values you have identified in your self-assessment. Reviewing the profiles of the faculty at the schools of interest is another way to see whether the program has faculty with expertise in your fields of interest. You can also arrange to meet with resource persons within the faculty and with alumni or current students in the program to discuss your questions. Do not forget that with each contact you are marketing yourself at the same time you are seeking information. The next section of this guide—Phase Five of the Model—offers specific marketing tips and strategies.

Use your self-knowledge and your career vision to assess congruency among your values, interests, learning style, career goals, and the various graduate programs. You can then more accurately assess how well any program will help you progress toward your career vision. This is where knowing theoretical bias and teaching/learning approaches among other program characteristics can help you make a decision that is a good fit with who you are, how you learn, and what is important to you. At any stage during this process, it can be helpful to seek the perspective of your mentor, student colleagues, and significant others. It can also be beneficial to speak with students you know who are currently engaged in a graduate program or are recent graduates. Informal sources of information and guidance are often valuable resources as you prepare for your graduate education.

As you can see, using your strategic career plan to help you prepare for graduate studies prompts you to revisit all stages of the career planning and development model with a specific focus in mind. The work you will do as you explore graduate studies illustrates the dynamic nature of the career planning and development process and how it guides you in your efforts to achieve your career dreams.

What Have You Accomplished?

You have a game plan! You have used your environmental scan, your self-assessment, and your vision to develop some plans that you can begin now. You have a concrete place to start. Your vision is on its way to being a reality.

What Is Your Next Step?

It is time to start telling others what you have just confirmed for yourself. You know your current strengths, values, interests, and accomplishments; you know how they fit with the world of nursing; and you have a plan. Now you need to share all of this with the people who can help you.

PHASE FIVE: MARKETING YOURSELF

Student Nurses as Self-Marketers

Marketing simply means being able to communicate confidently and effectively to others your strengths, interests, and goals, as well as the contributions you can make to professional practice. What better place than your nursing education to acquire self-marketing skills?

A third-year student made the following comments about self-marketing:

> Although I was already aware of the importance of developing a career plan, I learned that the process does not end there; rather, the plan needs to be put into action through the use of various self-marketing strategies. I want to make sure I get the job that is right for me. For this reason, I feel it is important to implement appropriate self-marketing strategies so I can represent myself in the best possible way.

The key to successful marketing is to develop an approach that is congruent with your values and communication style and true to your abilities. When you completed your self-assessment, you identified your values and beliefs and evaluated your expanding nursing experience, accomplishments, strengths, and areas for improvement. Now that you have taken a close look at the things that make you unique, you can most effectively promote yourself by making and keeping yourself visible to help you meet your goals. Your strengths, coupled with a commitment and belief in yourself, make you your own best marketer.

Why Marketing Yourself Is Important

Intentionally or unintentionally, you market who and what you are in every professional encounter. During each clinical placement experience, each involvement in the classroom environment, and each meeting with a faculty member or student colleague, you communicate (directly or indirectly) your values and your professional identity. Thoughtful and intentional self-marketing enables you to take control of how you represent yourself to others. In this section, you will learn about the resources and tools that form the foundation of an effective self-marketing strategy; you can then use this strategy to create your own opportunities.

How Can I Market Myself?

For student nurses, self-marketing is facilitated by establishing a network, acquiring a mentor, and developing written and verbal communication skills.

Networking and Support Groups

Establishing a network is a fundamental step in self-marketing. Networking can serve many purposes for nursing students. It involves meeting with a variety of people who share similar interests, practice in areas of nursing that are attractive to you, and can offer new ideas, perspectives, and opportunities. Besides being a valuable way to establish and maintain your sense of professional identity, networking also offers the opportunity to inform others of your interests, activities, and hopes for your future practice.

Networking can produce significant results if you believe in yourself and are committed and prepared to work at it. Be mindful that your networking activities will likely become more focused as you progress in your educational program. Initially, you may feel unsure about the most appropriate place to start to network. Until you are ready to choose a specific focus for your nursing career, it may be most beneficial to concentrate your networking activities within your school of nursing. As you start to develop some questions and focus related to your career interests, you can benefit from networking resources in the broader nursing community.

Throughout your nursing education, but particularly in its early stages, it is important to discover who your classmates are and how you can establish a sense of involvement in your school of nursing. Meeting students at all levels of your program will help you to find others with similar goals and interests. It will also offer you the chance to find out about interesting courses, clinical placements, and resources—not to mention the support that you could enjoy through your interactions with others who are experiencing similar challenges and adjustments. Becoming actively involved with professional student groups is an excellent way to meet student colleagues and provides many advantages, including the following:

- The opportunity to meet and work with a large number of faculty members
- Support in attending conferences and workshops locally, provincially, and nationally
- Opportunities to gain experience in working on committees and in public speaking
- The development of overall leadership skills

The first step in developing your own network is to make a list of people you think may be helpful to you. Consider all the facets of your life as you identify potentially helpful people—social life, family life, school life, and work life. In addition to student associations, faculty members represent another opportunity for networking that is "at your fingertips." Each faculty member has recognized expertise in one or more areas of clinical practice, research, and education. The exchange of interests and ideas can be mutually rewarding for you and the faculty member.

The process of networking with your classmates can be both formal and informal. Joining student groups and committees is one formal means of meeting and working with fellow students. A fourth-year student described the following example:

> I became active with student groups within 2 months of starting nursing school. From there, things just blossomed until I was making connections with students on a national level through my professional nursing students association. Now that I am ready to graduate and look for a job, I have a network of colleagues I can call on for advice and direction.

Involvement with the student nurses association allowed this student to meet others both within her nursing program and from other nursing schools. The many advantages associated with becoming involved with formal student groups in the academic setting include (1) the opportunity to meet and work with a large number of faculty members; (2) support in attending state/provincial, national, and even international conferences and workshops; (3) opportunities to gain experience in working on committees and in public speaking; and (4) the development of overall leadership skills. Whether you choose formal or informal settings (or both), such involvement means networking with your peers; sharing your vision, goals, and interests; and allowing them to keep you in mind as they participate in their experiences. You, in turn, can do the same for them as you encounter new experiences.

The exchange of ideas can be a mutually rewarding experience for you and the faculty member. One student reported the following networking experiences within their schools of nursing:

> In my final year, I volunteered to be my class representative for student council and also became a member of my school's nursing honour society steering committee. These opportunities allowed me to learn more about faculty members and to interact differently with them from the way I would if we were discussing a test grade or paper. The faculty offered guidance, resources, and support.

Another excellent opportunity for networking is through volunteer activities. The people you meet during your volunteering will help expand your network. Volunteering serves as an opportunity to develop new skills and to gain experience and insight into a new environment. A good place to start is in your School of Nursing. Many faculty and fellow students are involved in committees and organizations and would welcome new ideas, energy, and enthusiasm. Your career vision can also help you to identify volunteer activities. For example, if you are interested in working with clients in palliative care, you may consider volunteering on a palliative care unit. The time commitment required for volunteer activities varies, so you need to check whether you can fit outside volunteer activities into your academic schedule without putting undue stress on yourself.

Once you have established your network(s), you can target certain individuals and begin to build and maintain a support group. Your support group can consist of fellow students and faculty who believe in you and want to see you succeed. Surround yourself with individuals who keep a positive attitude and are a source of confidence as you develop an action plan to reach your career goals. Seek out those whose feedback you value and whose emotional support you can count on, particularly when you take risks.

You may want to build your support group right now. As you engage in the career planning process, a support group of your peers can help you explore your options and problem solve as you work with the model—and network!

Finding a Mentor

The second step in your self-marketing strategy should be to acquire a mentor. A mentor is someone who takes a personal and professional interest in your professional development. Your mentor will guide and support you through all areas of the career planning and development process as you transform your dreams into reality. In the nursing world, mentors generally are experienced nurses who know the ins and outs of the health care environment, have more connections, and have more access to information than less experienced, often younger, nurses. Do not restrict yourself to the nursing community to find a mentor. Your social and community connections are also excellent resources.

Determine the source and type of mentor you need by looking at your self-assessment and considering exactly the type of help and support you require. Through coaching and moral support, your mentor can help you scan the environment and give feedback as you assess your own strengths, identify your career goals, and develop a career plan. Of course, not everyone needs or wants a mentor. However, mentoring is another valuable way to ensure your career success—so consider it.

For nursing students, a mentor may be a faculty member who has taken a special interest in you, has influenced your career decisions, and has helped "open doors" for you. You may also encounter nurses in your clinical experiences, summer employment, volunteer activities, and other professional activities who represent role models for you. Once you have identified a possible mentor, create both informal and formal opportunities for each of you to get to know one another. Such opportunities include volunteering to work on similar projects or choosing to sit on a committee in which the mentor is a member.

A fourth-year student described his relationship with a mentor:

> My clinical advisor from third year has become an excellent mentor. We have had numerous opportunities to work together, and she has a good idea of both my strengths and my limitations. She has provided me with advice and support regarding my career direction, and she has suggested other individuals I could meet with to discuss my interests. I feel that working with a mentor is a great self-marketing strategy that I can continue to use long after I graduate.

Another student described her mentor in the following way:

> She was an influential faculty member who took the time to assist and get to know me. She identified opportunities for growth and encouraged me to explore them. She provided opportunities for me to be involved both within the school and in the broader nursing community. I learned from her professional presentation, and she seemed to take extra time to help me with my professional development.

A senior student described her experience in asking a faculty member to be her mentor:

> I really enjoyed the clinical instructor I had in my medical-surgical placement in the second year of my program. Even in her role as an instructor, she really seemed to make a difference to the patients. She also got along well with the staff and was involved in a lot of professional activities. I often thought that I would like to be just like her when I got to be a "real" nurse! I never told her that I admired her; I just assumed she would know that. In my fourth year, she was my clinical advisor for my final placement. She was still as active and as impressive as I remembered her to be. I decided to tell her that I considered her to be a great professional role model. I also asked her if she would be my mentor. To my surprise, she said that she would be honoured to act as my mentor and, since that meeting, she has already begun to inform me of activities and people that she thinks would be helpful to my career.

Developing Your Communication Skills: Marketing Yourself on Paper

Creating a targeted résumé and other written communication (e.g., business cards) is an important part of self-marketing.

Résumés. Your résumé is one of your most valuable written self-marketing strategies. It is a summary of your skills and accomplishments. A résumé is also a way to monitor your progress in building the strengths and expertise that you have identified in your self-assessment.

Creating a résumé requires preparation, patience, practice, practice, and practice! Remember, there is no such thing as a "one size fits all" résumé. You must customize your résumé to ensure that it is effective for each specific opportunity you are pursuing. Use your résumé as a strategic marketing tool to accentuate the accomplishments, skills, and knowledge you identified as part of your self-assessment. It is an essential part of many clinical placements, as well as the job search process. You will need to collect some data about a potential placement or job opportunity before you can customize your résumé. Learn about the organization and the role of students in the organization and specific unit, and scan the environment to determine available learning opportunities and how your learning goals may fit with those opportunities.

It is helpful to have a "junk drawer" résumé in which to document all your clinical experiences (with a brief description of the skills and accomplishments resulting from each experience), nursing and non-nursing jobs, volunteer activities, extracurricular professional development activities, and professionally related qualifications. Create headings for all categories of activities (i.e., education, awards, clinical experiences, professional activities, professional memberships, employment history, and volunteer activities). If you find that you have headings but no activities to place under them, then you know that one of your career development activities should be related to that area of your professional life. When it is time to submit a résumé for a clinical placement application or a job, you can create a customized résumé by selecting the information from your "junk drawer" version that is most relevant to the placement or job for which you are applying.

A student résumé has three unique aspects: (1) the list of selected clinical placements, (2) the clinical experience summary and outcome skills and accomplishments, and (3) the documentation of past working experiences, including summer and part-time employment. The list of selected clinical placements includes those clinical placement experiences in which you developed and enhanced nursing practice skills and the knowledge most relevant to the job for which you are applying. Limit the list of selected placements to two or three experiences, with the description of responsibilities, accomplishments, and skills focused on those that relate directly to the advertised nursing role. The clinical experience summary informs the employer of the scope of practice experiences you have had within your nursing career. These experiences can simply be listed; include those completed in the early years of your nursing program and those that provided you with fundamental nursing knowledge and skills.

The components of a student résumé are illustrated in Appendix A. You may also download a résumé exercise and résumé template at http://www.elsevier.ca/DonnerWheeler/ to help you begin to build your résumé-writing skills.

Your résumé should always be accompanied by a one-page cover letter. The purpose of a cover letter is to encourage the recipient to read your résumé more carefully to determine how your specific learning goals, experience, and abilities fit with their organization or society. It should be written on personal letterhead paper and attached with your personal business card, which together provide all the details the reader needs to get in touch with you. An example of a cover letter can be found in Appendix B.

Business Cards. Business cards provide a professional and simple way to introduce yourself to others and to ensure that they do not forget you. Student business cards need only have your name, phone number, and e-mail address. As one student observed:

> I never thought it would be appropriate for students to carry and distribute their own business cards. After a career planning and development workshop, I went home and designed one with a computer program I have. I think this strategy is an effective and creative means of giving others a way to reach me by telephone, fax, or e-mail. I included only my name, the fact that I was a student nurse, my university, and contact information. I was encouraged to keep the card simple, and it looks great. Having my own business card also makes me feel more professional and important.

Developing Your Communication Skills: Marketing Yourself in Person

Each time you meet someone new, you are presented with a marketing opportunity to accent your positives, take credit for your accomplishments, share your professional goals, and remind others of what you have to contribute. To seize these opportunities effectively, you should rehearse a short self-promotional statement. Then when you meet people and are asked to talk about yourself, you will be ready to clearly, concisely, and confidently articulate your current level of knowledge and skills, your present and future career goals, and your unique contributions. You do not need to wait for people to come to you. Become active in your school, student and professional associations, and interest groups, and contribute to an initiative that will help you both build and profile your talents and accomplishments.

The Interview. The interview provides another excellent self-marketing opportunity. You will need finely honed interviewing skills whether you are interviewed for a clinical placement, a job, graduate school, or a volunteer position; by a professional association, or by a community agency. Interviewing is a powerful self-marketing opportunity to present your interests, knowledge, skills, and potential in the most positive and appropriate manner.

Many clinical agencies now require that students participate in an interview before being considered for a clinical placement. You should plan for these interviews as thoughtfully and thoroughly as you would for a job interview. If your self-assessment, career vision, and strategic career plan are up-to-date, and if you have done your preparation, your chances of enjoying a successful interview are high. At the time of the interview, it is important to have clear learning goals based on your self-assessment, nursing program objectives, and knowledge of the clinical setting.

Your answers to the interview questions can demonstrate that you have relevant interests, entry skills, knowledge and, most important, the enthusiasm and ability to learn and make contributions to the placement unit. The interview also gives you an opportunity to have your questions answered so that, if you are offered the position, you can consult with your mentor, clinical placement coordinator, or clinical advisor to make a well-informed decision about whether the placement is the right one for you.

> In preparation for an interview at a clinical placement agency, Janet obtained (1) copies of the philosophy of the unit to which she was applying, as well as of the nursing department; (2) a copy of the hospital's strategic plan and an RN job description for her clinical area; and (3) a schedule of selected professional development opportunities she could take advantage of as a student in the clinical placement setting. She then spoke with two students who had experience in that unit. Finally, she met with her mentor (a faculty member with expertise in her chosen clinical area) to discuss how the skills and accomplishments identified in her self-assessment and her related learning goals fit with available learning opportunities and the philosophies and plans of the clinical unit and organization. Janet also participated in a mock interview with her mentor before her clinical interview.

Check http://www.elsevier.ca/DonnerWheeler/ for an interview exercise to help you build your interview skills.

References. Faculty members, mentors, clinical preceptors, part-time and summer job employers, and contacts from volunteer activities can be appropriate sources of references for students. It is important that you select referees who are familiar with your current level of clinical skill development and recent clinical accomplishments relevant to the practice area to which you are applying. If a referee is not knowledgeable about your recent work, provide him or her with a copy of your résumé and any other information that supports your application for the job (e.g., self-assessment, vision, strategic career plan, clinical evaluations, completed clinical projects).

It is important to ask referees well in advance if they would be willing to provide a positive reference for you. After a job interview, offer the names of your referees if you would like to pursue employment with that organization. Contact your referees each time you give their name as a reference. Inform them of the specific requirements of the job you are seeking and any other information that will help them provide a comprehensive reference. Be sure that your referees have a copy of the résumé you submitted and any new information you have that may not appear on your résumé.

Self-marketing is about using all your resources to present yourself in the strongest, most positive way. Remember that the most important resource you have to shape your own future is you! Keep your career vision and goals in mind. Creating an effective self-marketing strategy that works for you takes time, effort, and patience. Following these strategies will contribute to realizing your goals. The following excerpt summarizes Janet's thoughts on the process of career planning:

> Learning about the career planning process motivated me to think more seriously about my career plans and what I have done, and need to do, to accomplish them. I have realized the importance of and need to clarify my plans and put them into action through a number of realistic self-marketing strategies. This experience has allowed me to be more self-directed and actively involved. I believe I have a better understanding of the numerous opportunities available to me and how I can take advantage of them in an effective way.

Complete Activity 6 to assess your marketing readiness.

Activity 6: Marketing Yourself

> Self-marketing is representing yourself in the best way possible by using all your resources.

- How is your marketing readiness? Use the following checklist to answer that question.
  - ☐ I know I am my best marketer.
  - ☐ I know how to network.
  - ☐ I have a support group.
  - ☐ I have a mentor.
  - ☐ I have a current résumé.
  - ☐ I have a business card.
  - ☐ I have excellent interviewing skills.

- Which areas need some attention? Develop a plan to address those needs.

What I Need To Do	When I Will Do It
1.	1.
2.	2.
3.	3.
4.	4.
5.	5.

What Have You Accomplished?

Congratulations! You have made your first tour through the career planning and development model. You have learned how you can use the environment, self-knowledge, your dreams, and your career plan to explore how you can influence your educational activities to meet your current and future career goals. You will return to the model again and again as you build your nursing career. We hope it serves you well!

WHAT NEXT?

Career planning and development is a continuous process—a "work in progress." To ensure that you are get the most out of your career planning activities, you should consider an overall evaluation of how it is working for you. Complete the following questionnaire after each clinical experience and on an annual basis. It will help you determine which phases of the model need more attention, updating, or more consultation and support. You can also use your journal as an ongoing record of how you are moving forward—as a student, as a future nurse, and as a person.

How Am I Doing?

Scanning
- ☐ I am aware of the current realities and future trends at the school, local, and national level *within* health care and the nursing profession.

Assessing
- ☐ I can describe my strengths.
- ☐ I can describe my limitations.
- ☐ I know how others would describe me.
- ☐ My current academic activities are a good match with my values, beliefs, knowledge, skills, and interests.

Visioning
- ☐ I can describe my ideal vision for my future.

Planning
- ☐ I can identify my career goals.
- ☐ I have a written career development plan in place.
- ☐ I know what steps to take over the next 3 to 6 months to further my progress toward my career.

Marketing
- ☐ I have established a relevant network.
- ☐ I have, or am considering, acquiring a mentor.
- ☐ I continue to develop my communication skills.
- ☐ I have an up-to-date résumé.

Choosing Your First Job as a Registered Nurse

Congratulations on successfully completing your nursing program! You have worked hard to achieve your nursing degree. It is a very exciting time to be a nursing graduate. The possibilities are endless, but excitement can be accompanied by anxiety. You have some important decisions to make. Many students ask the following questions:

- How can I make sure that I am choosing the job that is right for me?
- How can I sort out the benefits of one job offer compared to another?
- What types of questions should I be asking?

You are now ready to use the Donner-Wheeler Career Planning and Development Model to help position you to get the job you want. It is important to return to each phase of the model as you embark on the exciting process of choosing your first position as a registered nurse.

YOUR ENVIRONMENTAL SCAN

As you prepare to move into the workplace, it is important to update your environmental scan. Include a scan of national, provincial, and local issues and trends. The purpose of this scan is twofold: to determine the issues and trends in your particular area of interest/focus, and to inform yourself of the current realities and opportunities within the profession and the health care system in general. Current knowledge of what is happening in your area of interest will help you to get a sense of what is "out there" in terms of specific jobs, issues and gaps within those job opportunities, and what practice challenges you might be able to anticipate and reflect on as you revisit your self-assessment. Awareness of issues and trends in the profession, as well as in the health care system in general, will serve you well in the interview process. With this knowledge you can feel confident in responding to potential questions focused on what you see as current and future issues for nurses entering the workforce at this time. The scan can also cue you about questions you may like to ask in an interview.

If you know the agency to which you are applying, a significant focus of your scan should be learning about the mandate, philosophy, professional practice model, and resources in the nursing department. Obtain a copy of the job description to determine and then market how your skills, knowledge, and interests fit with the job requirements.

YOUR SELF-ASSESSMENT

Return to your self-assessment. It will not be the last time you do a self-assessment, but this is the one time that it will serve as a springboard to your first nursing position. Complete this self-assessment with a focus on your values, interests, knowledge, and skill related to your particular area of interest. If you do not have one area of interest, complete your assessment with a view to consolidating your overall professional interests, skills, and knowledge base. As you apply for specific jobs, you can refine your assessment to reflect the particular position at hand. In essence, you are streamlining your self-assessment to help you target the position you wish to secure. Undoubtedly, the process of completing your assessment will remind you of all that you have learned and of your identity as a unique professional who has much to contribute to nursing.

YOUR CAREER VISION

Time to dream again! This is an exciting moment in your personal and professional life. How have you envisioned yourself as a nurse? Use your vision to guide your choice of where to submit your job applications. How do the positions to which you are applying fit with your vision? Can you see the potential of the positions to help you actualize your vision? You have many choices as you move into the current health care system. You are needed and wanted. Your vision can help you make choices that fit with your current interests, needs, knowledge, and dreams.

YOUR STRATEGIC CAREER PLAN

Your strategic career plan can be focused on short-term and long-term goals related to getting the job you want. Your scan has given you important information related to opportunities and realities; your assessment has clarified your current interests, skills, knowledge, and values; and your vision is your future. Using this information as your guide, ask yourself what you need to do to meet your short-term and long-term goals and who can help you. You can focus your activities on getting more information, contacting resources, developing your résumé, or preparing for an interview.

MARKETING

Make an appointment with your mentor to discuss your graduation plans. Bring your mentor up-to-date with your career planning activities, and seek specific support to help you assess the relative merits of job opportunities. Your mentor can also assist you as you develop your strategic career plan.

If you would like to seek employment in your current clinical placement area, let your preceptor, clinical advisor, and nurse manager know of your interest. You have the information from your scan and your self-assessment to effectively market your interest and the contributions you could make as an employee in that setting.

Information from health care agencies can help you determine the fit between your interests and skills and the goals and philosophies of individual settings. An interview guide in Appendix C outlines the type of information you can seek when preparing for an interview. You can collect this same information long before the interview stage to help you decide if you want to consider a particular agency for future employment.

When you select agencies for potential employment, you need to customize your résumé for each employer. Review the résumé and cover letter sections of the guide, as well as in Appendix A, for tips on résumé development.

You *have* the knowledge you need to select the job that best matches your interests and your vision. You're in the driver's seat; enjoy the ride!

Do You Need More Help?

You have covered a lot of material. If it seems overwhelming, or if you are not sure you have a good understanding of it, your first step should be to go back to the beginning of the guide and review the material and activities. Then look at the references provided at the end of this guide. You can also join or establish a support group with student peers who are also using this guide to help with their career planning experience. Sharing your questions, ideas, and strategies can provide you with relevant support and new resources. Career resources within your college or university and faculty members with interest in career development are other supports available to you. The Internet is another valuable resource. You probably already use it a great deal to enhance your nursing education, but consider using it to find resources to help you manage your student career and make sound decisions about your future career. Of course, there are also nursing student and professional organizations that provide many paths to pursue learning and professional growth.

You are in a career with numerous and varied opportunities. Yes, there will also be many challenges, but armed with a clear understanding of who you are and what you want to contribute in nursing, you will be ready for that future.

I never lose an opportunity of urging a practical beginning, however small, for it is wonderful how often the mustard-seed germinates and roots itself.

Florence Nightingale

Career Planning and Development Resources

Beatty, R. (1997). *The interview kit*. New York: John Wiley.

Bolles, R.N. (2003). *What color is your parachute? A practical manual for job-hunters & career changers*. Berkeley, CA: Ten Speed Press.

Case, B. (1997). *Career planning for nurses*. Albany, NY: Delmar.

Donner, G., & Wheeler, M. (Eds.). (2004). *Taking control of your nursing career* (2nd ed.). Toronto, Ontario: Elsevier.

Foord, K.J. (1996). *Survivability: Career strategies for the new world of work*. Kelowna, British Columbia: Kirkfoord Communications.

Moses, B. (1997). *Career intelligence: Mastering the new work and personal realities*. Toronto, Ontario: Stoddart.

Moses, B. (2000). *The good news about careers: How you'll be working in the next decade*. Toronto, Ontario: Jossey-Bass.

Moses, B. (2003). *What next? The complete guide to taking control of your working life*. Toronto, Ontario: DK Publishing.

Sher, B. (1983). *Wishcraft*. New York: Dell.

Sher, B. (1994). *I could do anything if I only knew what it was*. New York: Dell.

Sinetar, M. (1987). *Do what you love and the money will follow*. New York: Dell.

Stovall, P., & Teddlie, J. (1993). *Student's guide to bias-free career planning: Opening all options*. Columbus, OH: Career, Education, and Training Associates.

Swartz, M. (1997). *Get wired, you're hired*. Scarborough, Ontario: Prentice Hall Canada.

Tallier, M. (1997). *Networking for everyone*. Indianapolis, IN: JIST Works.

Washington, T. (1996). *Résumé power: Selling yourself on paper*. Bellevue, WA: Mount Vernon Press.

Wickman, F., & Sjodin, T. (1997). *Mentoring: A success guide for mentors and protégés*. Chicago: Irwin.

Wood, M.J., & Ross-Kerr, J.C. (2003). *Canadian nursing: Issues and perspectives*. Toronto, Ontario: Elsevier.

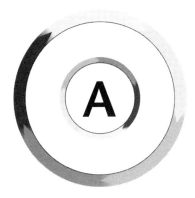

Appendix A: Samples of Student Résumés

Student Entering Third Year of Baccalaureate Program Seeking Clinical Placement in a Maternal Child Setting

Maeve O'Donnell
123 Four Street
City, Province/State Postal/Zip code
Tel: H: (123) 456-7891
E-mail: modonnell@coldmail.com
Fax: (123) 654-9871

Placement Objective: To develop knowledge and skill in family-centred care for women during the labour and postpartum experience.

EDUCATION

> **Baccalaureate in Nursing**
> Name of University
> City, Province
> Anticipated Date of Completion: May 2005

HONOURS AND AWARDS

> Member, University Chapter, Sigma Theta Tau International

SELECTED CLINICAL EXPERIENCES

> **Nursing Student, 2nd Year, Medical Surgical Setting**
> Worked collaboratively within a team nursing model to provide comprehensive care to adults in the post-operative period. Acknowledged for effective communication skills with clients and nursing colleagues, surgery-related client teaching, and leadership skills within scope of student role.
>
> Acquired Skills: Basic physical assessment skills, aseptic technique, simple and complex dressings, safe medication administration, therapeutic communication skills.

Continued

Nursing Student, 2nd Year, Rehabilitation Medicine
Worked effectively with preceptor in providing comprehensive client care within a primary nursing model. Acknowledged for strong communication skills with older clients, effective psychosocial nursing care, and basic physical care. Contributed to interdisciplinary client care discussions.

Acquired Skills: Positive therapeutic communication skills, effective body mechanics, health teaching, family-centred care, discharge planning.

PROFESSIONAL ACTIVITIES

2000-2001	2nd-year representative at School Council
1999-2000	1st-year representative at School Council

PROFESSIONAL MEMBERSHIPS

Student Member, Professional Association

EMPLOYMENT HISTORY

1999–
Present

Salesperson, GAP
Part-time position.
Required to work independently, providing supervision and training to new salespersons. Responsible for meeting consumer needs in a professional manner. Utilize effective organizational and management skills. Collaborative member of sales team.

May 2000–
August 2000

Personal Care Assistant, Lakeview Retirement Centre
Summer employment.
Required to work independently, providing basic care to residents. Utilized positive and effective communication skills. Acknowledged for strengths in conveying compassion, sensitivity, and respect to residents and families. Reliable and responsible.

VOLUNTEER ACTIVITIES

May 2000–
Present

Volunteer, Local Hospital Neonatal Unit
Help feed babies 2 hours per week.

Graduating Student Seeking First Nursing Position in a Mental Health Setting

George Donovan
1111 Twelve Street
City, Province/State Postal/Zip code
H (444) 222-3333; W (444) 555-6666
E-mail: donovan@nomail.com
Fax: (444) 777-8888

Career Objective: To secure an entry-level position as a staff nurse in the mental health arena, where I can further develop my clinical skills and contribute my growing strengths in therapeutic communication.

EDUCATION

1998-Present   **Baccalaureate in Nursing**
Name of University
City, Province/State
Anticipated Date of Completion: May 2003

HONOURS

1999-2000   Dean's List

SELECTED CLINICAL EXPERIENCES

Nursing Student, 4th Year, City Mental Health Outpatient Unit
Young Adult and Adolescent Client Groups.
With preceptor, co-facilitated psychoeducational groups for newly diagnosed young adults/adolescents with schizophrenia. Administered psychotropic medications and monitored the adverse effects of medications. Provided individualized client and family education related to illness and medication.

Acquired Skills: Administration of Mini-Mental State Examination, with supervision; facilitation of support and psycho-educational groups; individual supportive counselling.

Accomplishments: Developed a medication educational pamphlet targeted at young adults and adolescents.

Nursing Student, 3rd Year, Community Outreach Program with Focus on Homeless
Provided care to homeless individuals (e.g., foot care, medication administration, shelter arrangements).

Acquired Skills: Gained skills in engaging the homeless client, assessing health needs within the context of the individual's lifestyle, managing issues related to treatment adherence.

Accomplishments: Acknowledged for strengths in developing a positive rapport with hard-to-reach clients and in adapting care to the street setting.

OTHER PLACEMENT EXPERIENCES

2nd Year, Rehabilitation Medicine, Surgery, and General Medicine
3rd Year, Public Health
4th Year, Male Eating Disorders Clinic

Continued

PROFESSIONAL ACTIVITIES

2000-2001 Associate and Official Delegate of the Nursing Students Association
1999-2000 Year Representative for School Council

PROFESSIONAL MEMBERSHIPS

Professional Association
Student and Mental Health Interest Groups

EMPLOYMENT HISTORY

1998-2001 **Health Care Aide**
Summer Employment, Long-term-care facility, City
Provided comprehensive care to mentally handicapped clients in a medical centre. Responsible for direct daily care for five clients.

Accomplishments: Organized a family support picnic for residents and families.

1996-1998 **Waiter**
Restaurant, City
Developed skills in organization, time management, consumer-focused service. Provided competent and professional service to restaurant patrons. Reliable and responsible.

VOLUNTEER ACTIVITIES

2001-2002 Continue to organize annual family support picnic for residents and families of long-term-care facility.

Appendix B: Graduating Student Cover Letter

9999 90th Ave.
City, Province/State
Postal/Zip code
Phone Number

Date

Ms. Jane Smith
Program Director
Mental Health Unit
Metropolitan Health Centre
Any City, Province/State, Postal/Zip Code

Dear Ms. Smith:

I am writing in response to the advertisement posted on the Human Resources Bulletin Board for the staff nurse position in the Mental Health Program.

I will be graduating from my nursing baccalaureate program in May 2003. Over the course of my education, I have endeavoured to develop a wide range of skills relevant to mental health nursing. I have taken advantage of many learning opportunities with the goal of achieving strengths in therapeutic communication, psychosocial and mental health assessment and intervention, and interdisciplinary teamwork. I believe I have been successful in obtaining a solid foundation for mental health nursing practice. I would look forward to continuing my professional development in this area of nursing practice within your program.

My enclosed résumé has more details about how my clinical and educational experiences have prepared me to fulfill the needs of your staff nurse position. I would be delighted to discuss my potential contribution to your program and look forward to hearing from you.

Yours truly,

(Your signature)

Name

Enclosure: Résumé

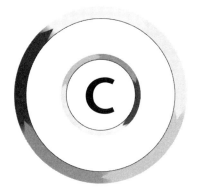

Appendix C: The Interview Guide

The interview provides another opportunity to market yourself. The better prepared you are before going into the interview, the easier it will be to promote yourself as the right person for the position. Thorough preparation also helps you determine whether this is the right job for you. Your self-assessment and vision are key as you prepare for and engage in the interview process. The following three steps are a part of the interview process:

STEP 1: PREPARATION

You will need the following information:
- Who is the employer?
- What is the composition of the nursing team?
- What is the job?
- What is the interview process?
- How long will it take?
- Are there stages (e.g., interview, short list, interview with committee)?
- What is the period for decision making?
- What is the starting salary?
- Is the workplace unionized?

ATTITUDE
- Create a positive feeling about yourself and your potential.
- Be clear about your skills and interests and how they fit with the job and the employer.
- Identify and contact potential references.

PLAN
- Develop a list of questions to ask the employer.
- Develop a list of questions you think the employer will ask you.
- Decide what you will wear.
- Decide whether you will take notes with you.
- Practice by yourself and with your mentor or a colleague.

STEP 2: THE INTERVIEW
- Be on time.
- Be positive.
- Listen carefully. If you are not sure you understand the question, ask the person to repeat it.

- If you do not know the answer to a question, say so, and indicate the steps you would take to obtain the answer.
- Remember that the interview is a two-way process; you are finding out about them as much as they are learning about you.

You may be asked the following questions:
- Describe your clinical experiences; what you have liked and not liked?
- Why do you want this job?
- What are your strengths and limitations?
- Identify something you have done that you believe has worked well.
- Identify something you would do differently.
- What are your short-term and long-term career goals?
- How would colleagues describe you?

You may have or want to ask the following questions:
- What are the organizational and nursing department philosophies?
- What are the unit/agency goals?
- To whom will I report?
- What are the professional development opportunities?
- What is the employee turnover?
- What is the orientation process?
- How long would I work with a preceptor?
- What is the staff mix (RNs, RPNs/LPNs, unregulated workers)?
- What are the next steps? When will I hear?

The interview usually consists of three components:
1. Breaking the ice
2. The "real" interview and information gathering
3. Closing the interview

STEP 3: FOLLOW-UP

If you are offered the position, you must evaluate the job and the offer and then make a decision. If there are some aspects of the job offer you would like to negotiate, now is the time. For non-unionized positions, remember that compensation includes, but is not limited to, salary and benefits.

Contact your references and let them know how the interview went and where their reference could substantiate or elaborate on your strengths.

If you are not offered the position, you may want to ask for feedback so you can work on improving your interview skills.

An interview exercise to help you build your interview skills can be found at http://www.elsevier.ca/DonnerWheeler/.